EVERY MAN I KNOW
IS A MAN I IMAGINED

l.s. browning

MY MIND'S EYE

[it is a mess in here]

my options are always
to create trouble or art.
i wasted no time creating the former.
now to transform
all that darling trouble into a
confession disguised as the latter.

INCITING INCIDENT

[incidental! not accidental!]

<u>invention</u>
do you think you'll write about this?
about me?*

<u>inventor</u>
of course.

<u>invention</u>
can i read it when you do?

<u>inventor</u>
absolutely not.

*i get asked this question most sunday
mornings. i have never had a clever response.
to turn myself into a liar, i've published it all.
now they can each read the things i wrote
while sitting on the edge of the bed.

DEAR READER

[endearment]

these are not love poems
they're intemperate declarations

violent words strung together with
neuroticism and egotism
and a bit of hopeless romanticism
(which i tried my best to get out in the wash)
but as they say; you are what you eat

and i gnaw at romance
like a middle child
in a freshly stocked pantry

they're not love poems

DIS-CLAIMER

[i mean it]

i will, on occasion, use the words 'men' / 'males' /
'boys' (and 'they' as an antecedent)

don't get emotional erectile dysfunction over this
broad brushstroke.
reread the title.
this is about the men i know and the men i imagine
(ooh trick phrase, those are two pretend categories
for the same group of people)

undoubtedly, i know great men. i'm related to them. i
have loved them. i've learned from them. i work with
them. i call them friends and mentors. i, at times, am
an adherent of men and have gone through phases
of my life dripping (to a problematic and distracting
extent) in adoration for the other gender (ew, but my
friends will tell you it's true)

here is an important distinguishing moment in my
arch as a woman,
i have never allowed myself to publicly dislike men,
to loudly say (without the veil of anonymity) that
the way i am treated by men throughout the day
is barbarically ridiculous, nearly incomprehensible,
and sometimes pure, wonderful magic.

it is a dichotomy that has left me weak-kneed, angry,
and disenthralled with remaining non-reactive.

so i am indulging in generalizations and the
occasional assignment of 'villain' to boys i want to
stick my tongue out at,
but i am also cloaking others with my gratitude and
my fascination . . .

<-

i'm sure you (kind contributor to my finances) are a
great guy (especially if you're a girl)
(oh no, making jokes already, are we?)

i assure you i will act like a proper gentleman from
here forward (obviously that means i'm going to say
whatever i see fit and justify it until you're dizzy)

PRE-PREACE

[delayed]

i am no longer tempted by the power of speaking at
a reasonable volume or the mystique of keeping a
neutral expression

i'd much rather untie myself
in a way that makes everyone as uncomfortable
as my thoughts make me
(loose shoelaces! how fun to all trip together!)

i'm not playing into the idea
that to be serious, i must not emote
(mostly because i find being stoic never leads
to an interesting night or a brilliantly messy day)

i reject
that softness and legitimateness are antonymous
or that a worthy mind
is one that only considers logic

both success and failure are pregnant with
the curiousness of how we interact,
with the volatility (and comedy!) of meaning
something and then meaning nothing to each other

it was necessary for me to assault the learned
sentiments that reverberate in my mind,
that my pursuit of emotional literacy is trivial
and not in line with my intellect,
in order to drain my feelings
into these pages
as if this book is a time capsule
of my soft years

ACTUAL PREFACE

[for real this time]

(just start the book already!
i know, but i'm bored and self indulgent
and trying to make a point about false starts and
maybe even an insane attempt to put you in the
emotional mindset of anticlimactic female pleasure)

you must understand

in reality
all i do is bleed in public
and cry in private

in fiction
all i do is start knife fights
and show up with spoons

if you think this is about you,
i pinky promise that it is
(i didn't write it in code, despite my promises to)
i've endlessly bit my tongue
for the sake of others
but at some point
one starts to worry
that the tongue may have other purposes
than being clamped between teeth

it would be timorous to not admit to the
convolution of loving
and hating
and none of it really mattering in the least

ORGAN-IZATION

[structure, but not logic]

divided by months and objects
(the pockets that i used to contain my wasted time)

and by fiction and reality
(the delusion that i used to cause my wasted time)

glued together
with hunger, solubility (ironically), and the
misappropriation of religion

april

it's april and i am
in fascination
and out of memory
plans dissolved
and rewritten
clothes off
i've never been this naked

i can't think clearly with
my clothes off
i should be made
to wear socks
whenever I make a promise

it was a slightly dirty erewhon bottle
that he held to his lips
gingerly, but void of trepidation

it was the way he knelt on my bed
(so few men can sit on their knees)
(i wonder how they pray)
staring at me like i was a craved for answer
to a question he hadn't been brave enough to ask

it was that
and the words that escaped his thin lips
as he stood on my couch,
at an hour we should've been sleeping,
a detective of the parts of me
that i had hidden under glass

i enjoyed him selfishly
it was all about me
and the way it felt to let him wear my body
the permission i gave stemmed from
narcissistic intentions

using only his hands as encouragement
i felt re-found
put together
by a revolving door
that i knew not to count on

i wanted to pump the night full of preservatives
and turn our collision into a fda nightmare
unhealthy but with the longest shelf life possible

grief for my adolescent form:
the widening of my hips
splintered my future expectations in a similar way
that my skill in the kitchen
and my tact with children did
a fog over my atypical ambitions and plans
betrayed by my natural skill set
and developing body
this is the part of maturing into adulthood
that i want to fight the most by
spending nights pounding my wide hips with my fists
and whispering to myself that children are parasites.
i feel as if i have not yet started to live
before the structure of womanhood wants me to
sacrifice for a man and a child.
i am in constant need of mothering
and pulled apart by the fact that my body looks
prepared for the reverse,
with its pesky monthly reminder of a purpose i
never asked to be painted with
it makes me ache for my girlish hips
for the flatness of my chest and the toothy grin that
only can occur in the years before you realize the
way men who have never heard you speak will look
at you with the desire to implant with their future

these are the days that you escaped death,
sharpened your teeth so you could eat raw meat,
and stopped taking your vitamins

defiance against needing anything that wasn't
already inside you

at twenty four i learned
an unused (yet second hand) kind of intimacy
when your pink striped pajamas
replaced my old t-shirt
handed down elegance
like a big sister and lover and best friend all in one
a silk secret that i wear whenever i raise my
eyebrows at men that i intend to make my yo-yo
emboldened by wearing your feminine outer shell as
my own and whispering phrases into their ears only
so i can watch you smirk when i replay the tape
recorder of my actions for your nod of approval

sunroof screaming
through the desert
and down hollywood boulevard
the way we ran on pavement at night
and stumbled slowly
on the same streets the next morning
breakfast at sidewalk diners
the only thing you've ever let me buy you
is ice cream
several times over
i swear i wasn't delusional
because i remember the look you gave me
across the overpriced t-shirts at the los feliz flea
and the strange way you described your style
and the fact that
the first whole day we spent together
you had a pimple on your forehead
and i wanted to tell you, but i didn't
you remembered everything about my tree
and nothing about me, so that each time i could
retell you the facts of my life
and after all of that doing
and remembering
and being
the way we acted
like i was meant to be effaced
without guilt or sadness
we disbanded what had no flaws
and didn't tell each other why

let me show you my point while i explain it:

i seem to only be capable of speaking in
contradictions as of late.
as if to signal
that i'm doubting the existence of truth
which puppeteers my brain to say so much
but nothing at all
a form that erases itself
like invisible self reverence
an unprovable commitment to the rule
a fear of staying silent
met with a need to not be heard

in other words, this poem

may

i was habitually in
the bathtub
being electrocuted
(by her)

french music and
overpriced candles
life was
disproportionally
luxurious
i didn't spend any time
under fluorescent lights

bracelets made out of your thumb and middle finger
worn exclusively in the middle of the night
you're the only reason i'd agree to sit somewhere
besides the driver's seat

the street lights have not yet slowed down
to catch the moon
it's redundantly bright

there is a man that i'm about to meet
a man that i already covet
who stands under the streetlight
and the sunshine all at once

he knows where i keep my water glasses
and which side of the bed is mine
he knows all of this before he has met me

when the moon is out,
when the streetlights have correct timing,
he will be gone
but he'll still know which side of my bed
i'm sleeping on

i was captured by how you defy death
and cover my torso with it at the same time

zipless
& permanent
& other horrible contradictions
that i'd rather not admit

we are dysfunctional
and i am utterly comfortable
because the correlation between
deterioration and effort
parallels how each new day of adulthood feels

the year i no longer felt fear:
all the bad things happened
and i lost my mind
and my tea still tasted like i expected it to

the first thing that nailed me to you
was how you made me feel 3d
like you wanted to construct an idea of my past
in order to understand the things
i was telling you in the present

june

i kept myself satiated
by saying
'i'm on my way out'
and collecting
new smiles
that had short life spans
reveling in the fact that
the promises weren't
empty, they were dead

i threaten my future
with my fondness toward things
and people that erase me

i cannot stop myself from going back for more of
less-of-me

it is comfortable to be nothing and have nothing to
become, to be eclipsed by someone
who seems larger than your plans

it is a way to waste an entire life

a tempting one at that
when the work at creating self is taxing and isolating

the inverse of a writer being unwritten:
a birds-eye-view of me scribbling
down the details of my life
but what i'm writing is actually about him,
nothing about me at all
erasing my own time with how i've shoved my
energy into his pockets

geographically and emotionally
you are my apricitiy
on the other side of the world
laying in the sun while i button my coat
i like to think of us as children
playing in opposite climates
sand castles and snow angles
thawing our ice and freezing our sweat
every verb that i did with you was candied
the memories of which have been bottled and saved
labeled with doting words
and put on the highest shelf
i'll mail a post card to new zealand
and marvel at the fact that i have you to send it to

you're a drug not a man
i feel milked
like all i can produce
i have produced for you
it's a daze that disorients me as i'm
intoxicated with our connection and
tempted by a future
that has no foundation

i do not recommend scribbling
a strategy on the inside of a medicine cabinet
you'll never be in a clear state of mind
when you're trying to reread the notes
created by your past decisions

you must love the annoying & mundane &
wednesday morning, out of milk, burnt toast of it all

it is not a crush. no. it is a crushing desire to
consume (you). a need to invent self as other, to
mirror, and to hold until i disintegrate and you
disintegrate and finally we can become something
that resembles all of your future and none of my
past. i crave your cynical nature being my own. i
want your ability to cut life with your teeth and to
overturn the table when you no longer want
what is being served. i'll master the way you walk
just in time to perform my stroll to the stairs.
when you come looking for what you've lost, i'll
remind you (in a voice shockingly similar to your
own) that we were never in love, just obsession, just
in compulsion need for the escape into each other's
polarity. i will not be a guest inside your personality.
i've bought it and own it and will never give it back.
does it count as assault? to take someone's attitude
as your own without their permission.

i sat down to write about how i wake up and gag on your name. but then a particular french song came on and the sun reached my favorite spot in the sky and a stranger's smile offered me a dangerous amount of encouragement. so maybe i don't need to say what i wanted to say. but if i was to say it, these would be the words i used: i'm writing three novels, all of which have your name as the first line. i was going to say that i wish i could put my words on a sugar free diet—that i could make them appear as something not dripping in sweetness, because then i could match your coldness. but i am wiser than to think myself capable of the sterile, stiff language of your world. i just accidentally killed an ant and am holding back tears. i have no chance of mastering your cool breeze. i was going to say that i've become increasingly convinced that the meaning of life is nothing at all and somehow this belief has increased the need i feel to make you a flower crown and teach you how to make dandelion soup and mud pie. there was much i was going to say to you before the song, the sun, and the stranger. so now, i'll keep my lips pressed and skip off to cause mischief in a place where i feel i can hide from the memory of and longing for you. did i write this today or 8 years ago? it is all the same isn't it. the whole world is spinning, not just me on my merry go round.

i will teach you how kissing can be a language
but you must let me run away right when the lesson
is complete

in the end
i did teach you the language of kissing
but it was you who taught me how to run away
i kept acting like i couldn't find
my keys or my shoes
until you threw them at me
and i could no longer fake ignorance

gently tell me hard things
whisper to me until you have outed
all my shortcomings
and i'm forced to grow up
so that we can be together
in the world of actuality
instead of the pretend safe haven i've
been wistfully creating

when my rights were taken away
i put on my dad's old sweatshirt and jeans
to feel the safety of external masculinity

on my seventh trip of the year to the gynecologist
i wore a men's button up shirt and tie
as if
the presentation
of manhood
could counter balance
the blood i felt on my female form
every time words like cancer and test and
swab and deep breath and it's going to be cold
were spoken

i know you don't think love is real
a point to which i don't feel impassioned to disagree

but this is what i think it is (the special thing
happening between you and me):

having a reason to buy a full sized red onion
and a sounding board for discussing the things
we were taught as children

i will not say i love you
but oh how i large red onion you.

july

bodies of water and
bad choices
desperation as a map
swatting away all
hands of deliverance
yelling to everyone
that it was fun not a
fever

letting people pretend i
was theirs
to have as long
as they acted,
at the height of
their pleasure,
like they couldn't
remember my name

to the boy who can't eat fruit:
you were the anchor i had always wanted
but entered my life, inconveniently, the day i
announced i was heading for the sea

there was an infinite gentility in the way
you forgave me for my plans
and a magnetism in the way you weighted
the cons side of my leaving list

you made the edges of los angeles
into a playground & wrapped me in our silly rapport
i felt superbly immature when
our hands were superglued

the intimacy of our sporadic coffee shop visits and
constant grocery store aisles (did i ever tell you
that i fell down from indifference the moment
you offered to hold the basket) was untainted
and remains in my memory unfaded

i knew you weren't a threat
and you proved me right, endlessly and patiently
surviving off the little i had to give
in a summer of unknown, you became
my desideratum

nothing about you is jagged
nothing about you hints at entropy
endeared endlessly is what i am
to the way you
just wish you could eat fresh strawberries

you deserved
my fullness
(this is a notable first)

and maniacally
i couldn't make myself
into someone who could be yours to have

even though
i loved the way you chose to crave
not the idea of me
but my ideas

i was jarred by how different you were from your
surrounding company
like a cucumber in a candy store
so clearly the better decision
and in truth, the one i wanted to make

but i respected you too much
to bring you down to the level i knew i was playing
you were floating above me
it felt like being protected to have your adoration
and i didn't want to sacrifice it
with my collusion

so instead i tried to make a friend
out of a confidant
a rare collision
of 'i get it'

sometimes i want to be in the hospital
so that you have a reason to call

i think about crashing my car
just to have a story to tell you

something strong enough to
gauge your investment off your reaction

i could just ask
but i'd rather be sick for a week

i let you throw me into glass because
when you licked the blood from the resulting wounds
i could christen you as healer
and ignore the causality

i came home inside her
she was a room full of balloons that i could not pop
regardless of how sharp i made myself

constantly celebrating ourselves without any real
reason to except that we had found each other

it was a surfeit of what i was missing
during my adolescence
friend friend friend friend friend friend
i understood the word

a pair of pink leather pants bought as a bandaid
while i waited on bad news

she's the reason i stopped pretending like
i didn't grow up with dirt under my nails
and grass in my hair

august

pre-eminent and permanent
the new standard
for how i want
to spend my days
red sharpie runs
on sweaty skin
peanut butter budget,
but my wallet feels heavy
i love the taste
of saving money
and spending life
it was puberty,
if puberty had been
unblemished
baggy terry cloth
and eye contact
swallowing youth like
prescription pills
thinking our outbursts
of angst
would heal the boredom:
i could break my arm tonight
and still want to scratch
the record
to endlessly repeat this
tongue-on-the-blade plot
development

i want to replace my brain with a stone
and lay somewhere cold
so that i do not have to decide
between forgetting your name
or changing mine to match

i shoved my mouth full of replacements
so that i couldn't scream for you to come back
now i'm choking on distractions
while reaching new levels of malnutrition

i keep spending time with strangers because their
eyes vaguely look like knock off versions of yours,
a lousy attempt at an antidote for missing you,
the number of men that i've accidentally called your
name is embarrassing and tinged with shame
(maybe an accident,
more likely a bold act of 'let me pretend')

your name is the only sound that successfully
escapes my mouth when i feel anything similar
to the one thing i associate with you:
intense bliss that infiltrates my thoughts and
makes me want to twist into your combination of soft
skin and hard muscles pulled taught over the most
structurally sound skeleton of a home

(that was an excessive way to say: you're gorgeous
and i miss you and the replacements don't work like
the original)

i hope there is a spider in my hair the next time i see you. i hope that when i see you - whether it be at an airport or a train station, outside of a rental, or on the steps of your front porch - i hope in that moment it is raining and that we are both hungry. i hope you slept too little the night before and i have consumed too much coffee. i hope i get a stressful email as i walk up and that you have a missed call from your ex. i hope that there's gum on my shoe and that your nose won't stop running. i hope my white dress is covered in stains that i only notice when your eyes land on them. i hope your car runs out of gas and that the diner closes as we walk up. i hope that your neighbors are loudly watching a television show that abuses a laugh track. i hope that i trip on the curb and you stand still without smiling. i hope the ice cream melts before we can eat it. i hope you compliment the wrong parts of me and i laugh at the wrong thoughts of yours. i need the entire universe to conspire against us if i am to successfully remain on my side of the line that you've drawn between the tips of our shoes. i've never believed in this city's myth of sexy indifference, but then again, maybe i do, because my god do i believe in you.

september

anyone who was subjected to
spending time with me
in september
had patience running
out of their nose
i lost my mind and temper
& moral compass
there was no desire to search
for the discarded clarity
or kindness
in september, i carried
my knife everywhere
i threw plates, cried when
they broke, & then tried to kiss
them back together
porcelain chips covered
the ground
while i was running around
barefoot like i had done
nothing at all
turning 25 in the middle of the most
illogical string of gunfire,i was
armed & ready to fire at any sound
my goodbye was scarred
with my effrontery
i came up short when i tried
to pay for the graceful exit
everyone i admire gave me
yellow flowers
regardless of
how little i deserved them

i do not want to wake up to a rose in a glass next to a muffin on a tray awaiting me.

no. no breakfast in bed. no cut flowers. i want him to wake up to the empty space where my body was anticipated. i want him to smile and stretch out in the half empty bed. i want him to sleep in and roll over and feel the cold sheets against his legs as he is filled with the knowledge that i have once again taken off for the meadows. shoes abandoned on the porch. breakfast half eaten, dishes left to be done later. love interest in the bed — but not waiting. love interest getting out of the bed on his own clock to chase his own meadows and abandon his own breakfast. both returning after dark only to swap stories of sunsets and hills and fall asleep in a bed fully at capacity.

i need you to be out by the end of the night
but before you go,
could you tell me what it was like to reside so freely
and indefinitely in my mind all these months?
i bet you liked being in my morning thoughts the
most

because you're a domestic slut whose afraid that if
you admit it your sneakers and sunglasses will no
longer be enough to prove
your woke-liberal-man-ness

goodbye to you and your mess

it was a horrible use of time
(but in truth, i adored it more than anything ever)

i wonder if you'll wear those sneakers when you
marry her

i wonder if she'll be foolish enough to call you a
feminist

i became a cyborg
on my own
but because of you

i walked into the all night drugstore at 3am
on my own
and laid on the stiff vinyl bed the next morning
on my own
while strangers retraced
where you had been hours earlier

the nausea of reality not being in line with my plan
made me focus so intensely on not throwing up
that i didn't realize i was crying in front of strangers,
a thing i never do

sober on circumstance
drunk with confusion

you were assertively okay
with letting my body be classified as practical error
without my permission

none of this
would be happening
if the night before i had just been
on my own

time is not passing quicker in adulthood,
we are simply less eager for
what is on the other side of right now
because we have little conviction
in how we are using our days

only for you
have i done mental acrobatics
bending the things i believe
twisting the reality of your actions
to turn it into a story that people can root for you in

i took on your reputation as my social cause
i called it my offspring
a way to claim you
while you refused to claim me

we were horrifically unequal
but the same height
with the same corny smile
we found companionship in trying to sew the holes in
our broken dreams
with cold beach kisses
always using malibu as a get away car
sunglasses on and sunburns encouraged so we
couldn't focus on the insufficiencies
just underneath our skin
strangers saw our mismatched-ness
before i did
i was always getting asked what i was doing
with a rope tied between our waists
i didn't care to answer the intruders
we were too caught up in our relentless laughter
(always at a rude volume)
and with turning chatter into music
it wasn't grand
but at least it wasn't boring

october

i didn't know
i knew magic,
until i made myself
disappear.
i used the past to erase
my body
i hid in clothes
from a life
i had forgotten i owned
i only listened
to the cd's
we illegally burned
each other
a soundtrack of
innocence and best
intentions
i wanted to
lick the spoon
of childhood
completely clean

the most dangerous men are the ones who we
use as a tactic to avoid making our own plans

the way i play my indie rock too loudly
and lick the words as i scream them
pisses off the volleyball dads in their minivans
i watch the nastiness of their annoyance mixing with
their lust for my inhibition
i watch their hot-flashes through my rearview mirror
but all i can think about is how
you told me you loved me on this street
and i told you i wanted more mozzarella sticks

my love affair with how my hometown rejects me
is a poor use of thought
but it keeps me alive

i don't care about how your day was,
i'd rather you tell me
what you plan to change tomorrow

in my head on the road:
double fisting violent femmes and wall of voodoo
i slept on the floor last night but still my toothbrush
was electric
soon black coffee & ipa are going to start dripping
from my ears.
all i've been in the mood for lately is to put on my
nicest lingerie and play guitar hero
i feel the ghost of the pinky side of your hand
pushed against my collar bone

everyone else is getting serious. i am getting foolish.

the solitude was on purpose. it (almost) always is.

cards on the table. this deck isn't from the store.

i paid $7.50 for gas this morning and was consumed
with thinking about how many scoops of mint chip
ice cream i could've bought you instead

you can't throw your own funeral
only bite your lip on a crowded flight
and do your best
to dissolve in a way that leaves a stain

since i made the decision to entirely change my life,
every night i have had
the same dream of my exes
all helping me fake my death

it ends with me running barefoot
down a dirt road
as if heaven
is blisters and clouds of dust

november

i tried to survive on
transformation,
too much caffeine,
endless jars of olives,
and your apathy
toward me

i never got to tell you about the time that i flew to
texas and back in one day while you thought i was at
the doctor's office down the street instead.
i was waiting for enough time to pass that it would
become funny to you in the way that it was delightful
to me. i could go whisper it to your tombstone.
but i hate talking to dirt and bones.

i'm becoming too old for the number of dead people
i know to be interesting

tragedies become normalcy too
i can't make a fun fact out of the ending of
everything that was you
your absence no longer can be used to
justify my inability to start
i have to just be okay
with the fact that you've vanished
there's no intrigue
in someone my age
knowing as many dead people as i do
i feel morally ambiguous
in how much i dislike this realization

who am i if not a collection
of the un-lived futures of the dead people i know
(knew?)

i moved to london so i could smile a little less,
behave like a recently divorced rockstar a little more,
and mess up without the watchful gaze of those who
have expectations for me and the way
i politely exist in my mother country
in other words
i wanted to feel the power and reckless blaze of
being a male in his 20s:
inconsequential conquest of only things with
personal interest

as far as things that i've imagined,
nothing has been as impressive as you
i created you as an idea to escape
from the work of creating my own life

i invented a realm out of the shape
of your name inside my thoughts,
four letters that carved into my brain
like a branding iron,
a dimension of reality out of the potential
i imagined you to have

not only do you not exist
but we never existed
which means to kill you off
i also have to murder the version of me that i had
imagined next to you
the iteration of my growth and maturity
that never actualized
the children who will never have
our matching blue eyes,
the bikes that we will never teach them to ride

a mental action that feels antithetical and bursting
with vehemence because
despite my attachment to the concept of us,
regardless of my willingness to make my
consciousness an enceinte for the
best iteration of you,
none of this is what you wanted

you have taught me impermanency
(thank you)
and lunacy
(fuck you)

i wish i could introduce you to the version of you that i invented. you'd fall in love with him too. you'd be foolish and self sacrificing for him too. he's a religion for a faithless girl who believes in nothing except sucking in the air while we can.
i know he doesn't exist. but the mental figurine I've made of him feels like it defies time in a way that we could never. it brings me peace to think that he will always do the right thing while you and i will never be more than strangers.

i'd marry you before you could finish the question and then i'd regret it, joyfully, for my ever.

i wanted to absorb the girl on the train
i wanted to swallow her tiny nose
and bite her polished nails
and wear her smooth brown curls as my own
i didn't know if i wanted her to be naked so that i
could search for signs of salt on her skin with my
tongue or so i could steal her clothes
and wear them for a week straight.
most of all, i wanted to consume her naïveté
not the naïveté she had displayed but the naïveté we
assume of pretty people.
a myth their perfect bones do nothing to dispel.
i don't think the girl on the train and i
would've been friends.

what for so long i labeled as jealousy
is now blurry
i cannot blink the attraction away

everyone here has your nose
(which causes countless spikes in my adrenalin
while it's raining and all the hoods are up -
noses out ostentatiously on display)
how long until a nose is just a nose and not a sliding
scale of similarity to you

i keep trying to convince myself that you're both
married and dead

it's an average nose
and an absurd observation

as soon as there is a score card of
who has slit whose throat
and whose hands are covered in the remains of
stolen joy from the other
as soon as it is a fight between
how you've treated me and how i've treated you
then sex is dead and covered in earth
because it too
becomes a currency
for what we owe each other
as reparations
instead of a physical vocabulary
used to tell each other the ways in which
we're still alive

the gender studies major
didn't have a trash can in his bathroom
a fact that colored his long speech
about the nude, feminist art on his walls
with the taste of enemy propaganda
so i lied when he asked what i was reading
as if this minute rebellion would punish him for
claiming his name was cherries
when he responded quicker
to cough syrup

i ate carrot sticks while he did cocaine
he was the one with feedback to offer
i should be concerned
he said
that i'm eating food that's been
processed with chlorine
i was concerned
but not with my carrots
i was concerned that my early experience
was being tainted by an adult boy who could never
walk in a straight line
i wanted to be 5
and at recess
on a set of swings
i wanted to share my carrot sticks
and nothing else

a morning of hospital correspondence
followed by an afternoon of making no calls at all
my independence illness is flaring up again

a boy selling me pasta on the street asked how
many people i lived with
he wanted to portion it correctly
(and to see what his chances of sleeping
with me were)

just me

he said 'brilliant' as he handed me
a single serving of spaghetti

you have no idea how many jars
go unopened in my home
because if i can't open them
then no one will

i've started smashing them
and picking glass out of my food
it's a ritual i call 'fuck absolutely all of this'

a devil of a roommate is what i'll one day make
or i'll just remain my own nucleus and always have to
take my purse with me into the doctor's office

on the phone with nothing between us
except for miles and memories
i'm searching for signs of the person i had once
sewn myself to
and see only the ways that you are now
unrecognizable,
the thumb print of my work has
been scrubbed thoroughly off
i'm impressed and upset that i ever tried to leave it

a romance turned into a friendship
is a bit of a zombie occurrence

i'll take the dead eyes and bloody mouth
any day
if the other option is a clean cut

we never bought a first aid kit for our house, so the
enduring trickle of pain is fit for you and i

but old injuries get infected, and i'm scared that on
my wedding day, i'll still be trying to keep the red
result of your knife off my white dress

i will still be trying to pretend at optimal health so i
can convince another man that all my aches are
because of him and his weaponry alone

i'd do less hiding, less lying,
if i was covered in scars not scabs

december

december in london
was radically
unproductive
as i learned how to
dissolve myself
& let the
sticky solution
of my once-was identity
touch those
who came near

i've convinced myself that i like eating
dinner alone, and for the most part,
i really think that's true.
i thought that if i dissolved the
delusional side of my heart
(the side that believes in how nice life is when
someone hugs you while you do the dishes),
i thought if i could rid my mind of romance
that i could also dissolve you.
but no matter how many comforts i distill into
illogical & weak
& no matter how many of my fictional characters i try
to bleed the idea of you into, there still exists a spot
in my mind that knows no peace from you.
i've always found admitted danger to be more
sacred than any promise of safety.
give me the risk that is you or all my nights will be
unbearably soft & sweet.

i want to grip my finger around the injustice
and not let it escape before i turn it into anger.
not an anger that excuses
my laziness
but an anger that straps me
to my purpose

you kissed me for the first time
while i was disagreeing with you
about politics
in a tight corner
of a loud pub

you weren't kissing me to make me quiet
(an agenda that defaces my scrapbooks)
but instead
were kissing me because of the things i said
all it took was closed eyes and interlocked middle
fingers across the table for 25 years of accolades,
stickers, and good grades to melt from my memory
i fell into a vicious desire to constantly trade my
thoughts for affection
an exchange that felt like perpetual motion
but would eventually rot both the brain and the heart

i think we'd climb together
and fall separately

there is danger
when breath becomes a toy
one's survival
cannot be another's amusement
that's how cages are built,
lives are binned,
and wives are resourced

death to playing dumb
there is no winner in the game
of camouflaging your strengths
in an effort to intimidate fewer people

the impulse was to
dye my hair red
and only kiss girls
so if you saw me
somewhere dark
you wouldn't know
to call out my name
i wanted escape
from the way your
memory
curled around
my days
as if the payment
for peace
was the truncation
of my former self
a strange bargain
to offer
when no one is
trying to buy

penetrate me with your phd
i've been feeling empty of thought
like my eduction was a rouse
and my past accomplishments not an indicator of wit
but an act that everyone was in on
in agreement to make me feel like a contender
(they know that i cause less trouble
when i feel significant)
so now i look at you
a very smart boy
who wants me
a very pretty girl
and in the least self respecting way possible
i think your lust for me
could transfer your undeniable intelligence
that i could absorb your brain through my body
and eat your words so i could
spit them back out at you
and finally take myself seriously
all i have ever wanted to be
is a smart man
who soft women look at with envy

hayden's poem:

there is no glue or tape on you
nothing securing you to the pages of my catastrophe
no sticky past or promised future to bind you to
being anything in my life except a revered
friend of a friend

yet you decide to be soft in perpetuity
and to prove the existence of kindness
detached from personal motivation

you hand out smiles like the highway-shoulder-
flowers of my life and have asked
for nothing in return

dear friend, i hope life is as tender
with you as you are with it

a man is not a metal detector
you will not find the hidden worth inside yourself
by being near him

i am going to drown you in my success
i will form a web out of my accomplishments that
entangles you with no hope of escape
the only torture i want to subject you to is constant
and enduring reminders that
you couldn't thwart my plans
that no body part of yours was big enough to block
my path or divert my attention

on tuesday, right before i went to bed,
i caught on fire
i'm not being poetic
i really caught on fire
i laughed and went to the sink
my left hand in flames
with absolutely no one to tell
no one to say
'i saw it too'

i smiled while my flesh melted
unseen

one day someone will ask what the scar is from
and i'm not sure i'll be able to distill it into reality
enough to tell them

your tragic flaw is your need
to remove merit from sonder
before we age beyond our hearing,
i hope that you'll decide
to listen to thoughts other than your own

i let you ridicule the contents of my nightstand
i didn't mind
because i didn't agree
and your matter of fact belittling of my books
only made me laugh
i have never been insecure
about my psychic macrobiotics
i like what i feed my brain
much more than i like boys
i can digest literature
men, however, have very little nutritional value
after i consume them

on deciding that people are statues:
we're all just screaming
'we are here'
hoping to not run out of breath
before someone who seems
less finite, less dissolvable than ourselves
nods their head in acknowledgment
of our scratches on cave walls

we identify these humans who we think are made of
something stronger than ourselves
in the most arbitrary ways
i landed on you for no other reason than i thought
your music taste was well developed and i liked that
you touched my back while telling me
about a soup recipe the first time we met
the most illogical markers of stone

there is a facade of peace
that comes from thinking human union could be
stronger than the mammoths
it is empty and unwise to fall
into exaggerated meaning
(an unideal area of overdevelopment
that i know is oft my weakness)
the only thing that makes our hand holding
significant
is the thinking it at all.
the mammoths are gone.
we're not far behind.

the absolute violence (and kindness)
of you telling me that i'd be a good mother

i do not know how well i hid
the mental laps i started swimming to try to sort out
why you decided to say that
right then
when it was all falling off the cliff
and you knew resolutely
that i did not want to hold on
because i cannot live in a state of wondering
if i will ever touch the ground again

you swept me off my feet and
irresponsibly never reversed the action
i've been hovering and dangling and slipping

until that comment about the children i'd raise
and the way your emphasis made it definitively clear
that they would not be the same as yours

a call me out and tuck me in kind of love
i'll settle for nothing less

pray to me
i gave you the breath
that you used to resuscitate her
the greed in you disgusts me
your need to have one waiting
while another is being held
throwing both into a vicious cycle of addiction,
the way you have positioned yourself as the sun
in the solar system of the three of us
is repulsive and emasculates you in my eyes

your performance of guilt could be better
on your knees this time
and look up to me
beg for forgiveness with your tongue
buy me back
with your devotion as a tithe
make me your belief system
and crave to be made holy again
as if salvation is an option for you
do not use my name
but call me your deity instead
the hell you've put me in is the promised
land you should now crave

what i'm doing to you is admittedly cruel
i want you weak
so when i walk away
you're kneeling and helpless
the way i was the night we met

it was all over and i had no idea what was next. no thoughts. no plans. but it was sunny and i could feel my brain forgetting the details i had pleaded with it to remember. i felt like a mother who woke up without the responsibility of her child.
i was glad to no longer have to care for the atmosphere that i called loving you.

i bet your aunt has kind eyes
and no idea how you treat women

you're a joke

the punchline is that i was all in

this is how i cauterized the gash i cut in myself while
trying to get you out of my system:
i became unbothered by decision
on monday nights, out of preference
not impossibility,
i lock my door and stack my pillows to
be vertical instead of horizontal
(metaphorical without trying to be, but yes my head
is always higher when i'm alone)

i've made friends with
the graveyard cat
that little orange animal and i are living the same life:
existing alone
no longer trying to punch the things that haunt us,
letting people occasionally pet our bodies in
appreciation for how we jump
around on the dead,
trying to remind them how to be alive

the ending i want
is one that i'm reluctant to admit
because it means the feelings were candidly
unconditional

i want us to become strangers
only so we can
bump into freshly showered versions of each other
in a busy bakery on a sunday morning:
to lock eyes and lives instantaneously,
to get our fingers caught in each other's wet hair,
and to start again

this has a happy ending
dissonant, but happy.
not because i end up with him,
not because he decides on me,
but because i fall madly, egocentrically,
in love with the personal evolution
gifted to me by the rejection.
infatuated with the process
of being wrecked by my own desire,
and the resulting replacement
of plastic with granite.
a relationship with the unraveling of my plans;
bad news is my boyfriend now,
and we cannot stop fucking.

DATE &/OR DATA

[loose terms all around]

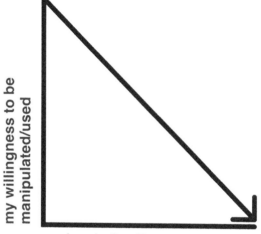

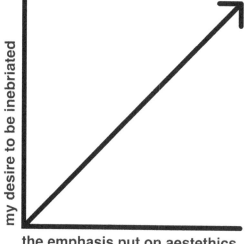

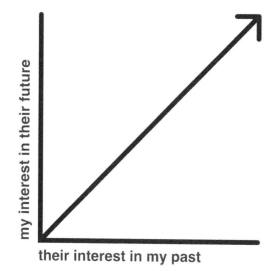

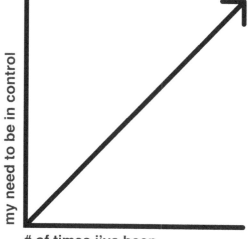

my need to be in control

# of times i've been
catcalled that day

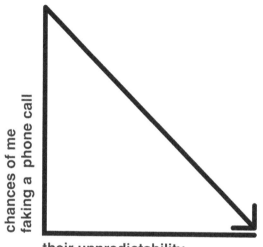

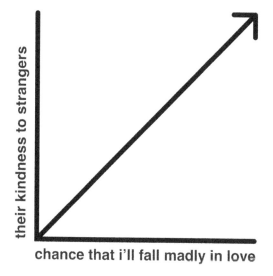

-FLOWERS +THOUGHTS

[an attempt to turn poetry into reasoning]

DE-GENDERING CHIVALRY

The correlation between equal pay and expectations of traditional chivalry.
The intersection of third wave feminism, egalitarianism, and economic etiquette.

Note: In this piece, 'you' will be in reference to a cis woman inside of a heteronormative relationship with a cis man. I am attacking a specific view of implied economic privilege that is degrading toward a female's own relationship with her view of self and is reductive toward her intertwinement with a feminist agenda. The tone is tough love because it is self critical and I am not an exception to the critique.

Equality inside of earning and spending cannot be viewed as mutually exclusive. I can say that in a cheekier way: if you want to wear the pants in the streets, then you have to be willing to wear the pants in the sheets. Expecting a man to pay for an entire date, for no other reason than that he is a man and you are a woman, implies that wallets are connected to genitalia and it regresses the progress made inside of the equal pay movement. The reasoning that gender determines economic burden, while dating, is riddled with obvious logical fallacies that I'm frankly uninterested in analyzing (I want to respect you as a reader enough to assume that you can understand the Swiss cheese of an argument that 'he's the man!' is when it comes to who grabs the bill). Without belittling your intelligence or delaying on this point, it would be irresponsible to not briefly touch on the danger that is applied to feminism in the action of this reasoning: when you yell 'he's a man' you're screaming 'I'm a woman' at an equal volume but connoting it with the inability to play on a level economic field and with the lack of desire to reach true equality; which entails not just the privileges but also the equitable distribution of burdens. I already find this analysis to be dull when a much more tantalizing question exists on the other side of accepting that equality is applied to economic responsibility.

The steamy question at hand is how, then, do we maintain the absolute, undeniable, sexiness of being taken care of, of being treated to experiences, of being adorned with gestures, gifts, and actions. Simply: how do we make splitting the bill sexy. We start with the root issue: the idea that 'chivalry' is gendered. The textbook definition of chivalry is that it is a noun used to reference the medieval knight system and the associated code of conduct toward morals, religion, and social situations. Here we can check the first box of chivalry being known as a man's game (women could not be knighted thus chivalry could not apply to them). If I right click 'chivalry' as I write this, I'm quickly offered 'gentlemanliness' as a replacement. Boom. We can check the box of our modern attachment of chivalry to men. The remaining definition of 'chivalry' however, uses genderless words that I, personally, hope to exude and be associated with in my relationships. These words include 'thoughtfulness,' 'attentiveness,' and 'consideration,' all of which are references to pillars of evolved, kind, and caring human interaction. If we can get over the initial hurdle that chivalry is in a man's toolkit, used only to win a woman (ding, ding, ding see the mildew of old misogyny already?), then we realize that splitting the bill or treating our date doesn't have to undermine the sexiness of his thoughtfulness.

Instead, we get to share in the game of considerate acts embedded with sexual interest and care.

This concept is larger than just the monetary implications, although that is the easiest distilled starting point because it is a rather universal occurrence. The concept can be extended to anything that falls into your individualized vocabulary of actions and gestures relating to care and/or romance.

Taking responsibility for equal effort of thoughtfulness liberates you, the female, from cookie cutter expectations of how to communicate value and worth in a relationship. Smashing the structure of: man provides economic security and extravagances, woman provides housekeeping and children, (the 1950's are calling and we could pick up if I cared about the causality of this tilted conundrum) opens opportunity for both partners to express their care in ways that are authentically motivated and not just traditionally regurgitated. Maybe you pay for dinner and the next night he cooks it while you sit there (I mean, really sit there. Not clean. Not help. Sit.) Maybe you buy him flowers (or something less trite, but tropes are helpful when making a point) and he plans the details of your next vacation. The theme here is that actions of attention and support are not, nor should they be, intrinsically gendered. Instead of, literally, buying into preconceived, archaic notions of which gender is expected to perform which communication of interest and investment, each partner should gravitate toward the chivalrous acts that are the most authentically motivated and the best tailored to their partner's needs. Girls can treat boys. Boys can treat girls. Actions of 'treating' become more meaningful when they are not expected or motivated from a place of stereotypical behavior and instead born from a true impulse of connection and effort.

By not allowing a man to pay for all aspects of a date, you are challenging him to find other ways to earnestly express his interest. By not allowing yourself to engage in experiences that you have no economic stakes in, you're freeing yourself from any subconscious behavior-owing-endowment. (The most typical allusion here would be sexual, but that's not what I mean. I mean that you are releasing yourself from the caretaker role while concurrently getting to feel the joy of equal economic power and influence).

I'll conclude anecdotally. While on dates I use to (somewhat forcefully) offer to pay as soon as I realized that I wasn't interested in the continuation of romance. Subconsciously, by paying I was freeing myself of emotional or physical investment in this person as currency for their shelling out of cash. Let me be clear here: no one ever owes emotional or physical services to another person because of any gift, purchase, or attention. Emotions and sex cannot be owed, only chosen to be shared. I am saying that I was unable to detach me egalitarian (maybe slightly communistically rooted) view of 'you did something for me/I should do something for you' from the structure of men paying on dates. I found myself allotting mental and emotional space to men as currency. This was a flaw in my own emotional maturity and reeked of my lack of self worth. I was only able to escape this self laid (and societally encouraged) trap of feeling indebted by leveling the effort up front regardless of interest, by empowering myself with the euphoric feeling of being the economic facilitator. By wearing the damn pants and being comfortable enough to call them a skirt. (This extended metaphor is my attempt to wash out the sexism in its parent metaphor).

The personal result was that I started using my real voice. Actually. My voice was lower. I stopped trying to dress sexy on dates. I started wearing whatever made me feel like the actual version of myself that was existent on that day. I stopped laughing at jokes I didn't find funny. I walked away when I was bored or unstimulated. Essentially, I stopped trying to be the purchased item of male attention. What I was left with was romantic relations that I felt like an equal fraction of. I watched the men I spent time with be challenged by this untraditional behavior and often bloom into kinder, softer, more attentive versions of themselves.

Removing gender from the process of courting, from acts of chivalry, and from expectations of dating allows both partners to naturally exist in their respective degrees of masculinity and femininity and furthermore to show up for each other in a more 'I'm-doing-this-for-you-on-purpose' way instead of an 'I'm-doing-this-for-you-because-it-is-expected' way.

THE ETHICS OF PRETENDING
PHYSICAL PLEASURE:
SHORT CUTS CREATE CONNECTION GLASS
CEILINGS IN BOTH HOUSES

I (have) fake(d) orgasms for two reasons. One: I went to etiquette school. Polite girls always make boys feel successful, obviously. (Don't worry, I'm in the process of unlearning politeness). Two: control.
(Maybe I should add a third: I'm a sucker for putting on a show).

In my early sexual years, I thought pleasure-based-white-lies had one victim (my lack of euphoria) and one survivor (enter sweet, albeit inept, boys here). I believed I could bandaid my complicated physical-mental need for simultaneous stimulation with a performance of congratulatory praise. I proved to execute this performance with such realism and convincing detail that the spectators always walked away with unearned smugness.

Faking orgasms gave me a secret that allowed specific ownership over my sexual interactions; the reality belonged to me and me alone, what my partners exited with was not my true experience, which made it feel like they couldn't walk out the door with any real part of me. It was like putting a fake memory in their pockets so they couldn't get through the doorway with something of mine. It felt like a buffer between body, mind, and vulnerability and a way to peacefully grab back the decision making I had lost while my clothes laid in a pile on the floor. If consent was a car, then the alarms would've woken up the whole neighborhood by now. Yet, I don't think my need to counter balance a loss of decision making was a result of a drastic injury or injustice (some minor ones, sure). I think young people often oscillate with how much they want to experience in their bodies. Faking orgasms was what I used to regulate. This was fairly harmless as a beginning tactic but soon proved to be worrying in its implications for the sexual future that was ahead. The habit was laying the groundwork for an adult sexual life that deprioritized pleasure and connection while placing personal control and isolation of experience at the top of my value hierarchy. It was a game of seeing how large of a delta I could create between my true sexual experience and how it was perceived.

The game was a coping mechanism for how worn out I was of men telling me what I was, what my skills were, and what I should or shouldn't do with those said skills. By 24, I felt like my existence was partially who I had been as a child and partially the adult woman that men had tried to shape me into. This is how I framed the feeling of having masculine ideation sculpt my impressionable form: (cis) men can't give anatomical birth, of course, so my postulation is that due to the absence of that ability, they relish the opportunity to give life to an untenable offspring that is half you and half the things they tell you you are. Lying about orgasms was my way of aborting the sexual accolades that were attributed to my person.

Once my brain and perspective matured, I was able to see how this weird mental game was arbitrary and pretend. I wasn't regaining self by keeping a single sector of sexual liberation chaste. More importantly, I had an ethical dilemma on my hands. I had been been misleading men for years about not only my experience, but about our connection. I was generally unruffled by my lies because I believed I was doing the boys a favor by removing the challenge and limiting the amount of time that was allocated toward me. What I was actually doing was putting a glass ceiling on my sexual experience, their sexual experience, and our combined potential for discovery of true, intimate connection and partnership. There is no intimacy without honesty. There is no collective gain without individual gain. There is no loss of power through the experience of pleasure. These are the things that I whisper in the ear of my adolescence whenever I feel muscle memory kicking in.

EMBRACING THE FLUIDITY OF ATTRACTION AS A TOOL FOR ERODING JEALOUSY

'Your girlfriend and I have decided we like kissing each other more than we like kissing you,' is an acutely misleading (and straight up antithetical) way to begin this, but the only way I know how to access the train of thought I'm aiming to dissect. This phrase about kissing someone's girlfriend came from seemingly nowhere and was stuck in my head August through November. I had no idea why. It felt like a secret and gave me the feeling of carrying a switch blade in the pocket of my mini skirt.

I was on a long flight and bored of all the books I had brought to read. Naturally, I decided to scroll through my pictures. I was mindlessly indulging in nostalgia when I was accosted with screenshots that a worse version of myself had taken. A memory that I had wiped clean from my recollection (such a convenient human coping mechanism for being able to relentlessly tolerate our own company). The Instagram accounts of 3 girls I once knew were saved like fossils on my phone. My clean slate of a memory was rapidly dirtied with old arguments and fiery flashbacks. Jealousy. It had been years since I had been as jealous as I was when I took those pictures.

The context is rom-com-esque: I was swimming in commitment toward the most wonderful boyfriend, we were young and addicted to helping each other survive, he was honest and kind, I was convinced that he was actually drawn to be with someone else (I had 3 potential candidates lined up), and horribly afraid that I was getting in his way of a more desirable relationship. It was all pretty harmless, but the distress that I sewed out of strange impulses and unjustified gut feelings was intense and illogical.

I readjusted in my airplane seat, somewhere over the Atlantic Ocean, staring at the pictures on my phone and feeling my cheeks heat up. Fire. But not the flames of jealousy. Without the stakes of a relationship and with the added years of experience and self-esteem, I was able to understand what had been at play in my hormone charged mind when I took those screenshots. The girls were beautiful. Not in the way I tell my friends they're beautiful, but in the way that makes the arches of my feet tingle and the back of my jaw tighten. A little laugh escaped me, as I pieced it all together. He wasn't attracted to these girls. I was.

I didn't know that I could feel that strongly about a girl's hair unless it was because I wished mine was more like it. The feelings of jealousy and attraction are wickedly similar; they both include admiration mixed with the desire to possess. Jealousy wants to possess the traits. Attraction wants to possess the person. In my immaturity and inability to correctly label the emotions, I had created a fantasy conflict that allowed me to constantly talk about these girls that I was magnetized to.

The phrase that had been echoing in my mind like an unused incantation came into focus. My 'haunting sentence,' as I had titled it, was not about some salacious act or the desire to corrupt a couple. It was about rerouting jealousy. This wasn't a massive moment in my life of fully redetermining my sexual identity or deciding on new terms with which to label myself. It was just a broadening of my self view that allowed for positive emotions where there had once been negative emotions. The dessert of growing up is when discovery can redefine something that was previously an assumption. You do the work of living and hurting and failing to be rewarded with a reveal of something that has been sitting inside yourself. I've become fond of thinking of the mental and emotional space of a 20-something as an advent calendar. It's all there...just not all there, all at once.

The notion that I could filter jealousy down to attraction opened an access point to unobstructed connection. My relationships with men became charged with a new clarity that allowed me to not invent reasons to be jealous. Jealousy could still find it's way between me and a man, but the change I was hoping to evoke with this emotional precision was the removal of contrived jealousy. It was a lucidity that took me out of the land of conspiracy and positioned me firmly on the ground of reality.

EVERYONE IS HOT FOR 25 YEAR OLDS

I once threw a party that no one showed up to and ended up eating the entire cake alone in my dorm room. This sounds like a sad story; it is not. It was one of the best nights of my life. Being 25 is the absolute opposite of that night. Being 25 is having a singular slice of cake that every man thinks you're bringing directly to him, even though you were planning on eating it alone. There is an acute violence in the assumed access that both older and younger men believe they have toward 25 year old women (this age may not be exact, but my best guess is most women have this experience somewhere between the ages of 23 and 27).

I felt the circus start September 13, 2022. 25 on the dot. Happy Birthday, don't go outside without a baseball bat and flexed middle fingers. (I'm kidding, if you've made it to the back of this book and think anything in me can stomach inflicting actual violence then maybe you're projecting a spine onto me that I wish I had. Thanks, but I don't go Harley Quinn on the random men I encounter on the street…I just fantasize about it). I've been crossing my fingers that the tent and all its clowns pack up and head out of town at my behest on September 13, 2023.

While trying to understand this insane occurrence, while trying to see what happened in me that catalyzed this grotesque out pouring of 'attention,' I started looking at my past, as is habit: turn backward when you no longer recognize your surroundings. Breadcrumbs, breadcrumbs, breadcrumbs. Nothing? Okay, land marks? Ah. Something. Not a clear connection yet, but land marks start to emerge that feel connected to my quest for context. I describe this current moment in my life as the time of whimsical brutality. I feel bizarrely prepared for it, almost like it was anticipated or natural (although still not acceptable). The landmarks that revealed themselves were all lessons in whim driven brutality.

The first lesson was taught while wearing a homemade CapriSun costume to high school. Fragile teenagers are cruel but it is nearly impossible to take insults very seriously while a giant straw is adhered to your head. The attacker looks more satirical than the victim looks weak. (Prepared!)

The second lesson was added under my belt while dodging the nerf gun fire of my brother's teenage friends—which was in its essence, playful violence. Learning to look at a man (if we can call the pimply, lanky, body-spray-soaked 14 year olds that) with a gun and laugh was helpful. In addition, this was a lesson in literal agility, in dodging, running, and ducking...smiling all the while because you know that you will come out on the other end alive, if not unscathed. (Prepared!)

The third was distributed through a recurring event throughout my early adolescence: constantly receiving religious items and monetary gifts from adults who I did not know and having to explain to them that I was not (fill in their chosen religion here) and was in fact a self proclaimed agnostic child. Even in hindsight, I cannot explain why this happened or why it happened with the frequency that it did. All I know definitively is that it taught me, shockingly early, how to reject people who were approaching me in an emotional state. (Prepared!)

The final preparation is only whimsical and brutal because of the age I was when it occurred and the irony of relationship. The first time my body was sexualized (to my awareness) through a male gaze, I was 8. Sitting crossed legged in the billowy pajama shorts I had just gotten for Easter (even agnostic kids love a good egg hunt). There was an overheard comment from my grandpa about how I should be corrected for my indecent behavior. Corrected for what? I was lost in the adult conversation and confused at what I had done wrong. A quick look to my older brother sitting next to me, in the exact same position. His reaction was always the thermometer I used to determine the temperature of a situation. My young mind acrobatically bounced between the nodal points of the room:

-my mom in full blown tiger mode pulling the old man into the hallway
-my dad's face reddening with in-the-middle-ness
-my atypically astute brother whose play had slowed down to cautiously gauge the stakes and subject of the adult tension
-my grandpa who, in my confusion, started to look more like an angry cartoon than a man
-myself and a feeling I had never felt before: shame. It was not a tornado. It was not an explosion. It was just an introduction to unintentional physical guilt and the twisting connection between your vagina and the back of your eyes when you're trying to not cry and unsure of what is causing the emotion. (Um. Prepared. Less fun than the others, but drenched with preparation for sexual harassment.)

I digressed from my original point, about the age range of men who try to grab your ass when your 25, to add this context because I had to understand why I was handling the aggression so calmly, out of concern that I was (oof, brace for it) enjoying it. When it first started to happen, I was running around Los Angeles, preparing for an international move. I thought maybe I wasn't being reactive to the constant slew of aggressors because I was distracted and tired and moving through space like a bullet. Then I arrived in London and it only got worse. 3 nights after I moved, I ran out to buy milk and peas. I was intercepted 5 times in 15 minutes. By the time I got back to my flat, I was appalled that I wasn't quivering or fighting back tears. Why was I taking it on the chin? This time I was worried that the (historically romanticized) accents were making me not register the threat of what was being spewed at me. This lack of being bothered made me feel like a bad feminist. Shouldn't I be spitting at them and kicking them in the balls, not staring straight ahead and continuing my grocery store strut like nothing had happened at all? This is where the gnarly concern that I was getting a visual self esteem kick back through abusive validation entered my brain and my journey back through whimsical violence began. After acknowledging how many events perfectly primed me for handling male harassment, I became less alarmed with my cool, calm, and collected ability to act like I hadn't heard them. I had been subconsciously training for this exact era.

In place of the oh-dear-god-what-part-of-my-repressed-self-is-flaring-up alarm, I had the space to get curious about the men who where flocking; more specifically curious about the range of men. Walking down the street and being approached by a 17 year old and then 5 minutes later by a 65 year old is an event that, if not analyzed, will make you feel like a free for all buffet of sexual desire. Partially the experience is strange because nowhere in my mind am I able to flip it in order to gain empathy. The idea of making sexual comments about a high schooler or a silver-haired retiree makes me physically sick. How could something so out of left field be happening so frequently? I was at a complete loss of an answer until months later I had an epiphany while on a video call with my best friend, a radiant woman; equally full of youth and experience. I stared at her admiringly; she appeared as a portal to all the things that are good. I wanted to adhere myself to her and breathe in the freedom she exuded. Ah-fucking-ha. I WAS BEING RESOURCED AS AN ESCAPE RAFT BY MEN OF ALL AGES WHO WERE TRYING TO CLAW THEIR WAY OUT OF THEIR OWN SHITTY SEAS.

The magic sauce of being a 25 year old, independent, joyful female is that you are loaded with enough adulthood to be a fully functioning, viable, societal contender while perfectly balancing a non desperate grip on youth, play, and naïveté. 25 is on both sides of the line of societal norms. You could be readily accepted as a wife and mother of 3. No taboo in sight. In opposition (at least in big cities), being completely unattached to a partner, family, or overly developed career at the age of 25 is also not generally offensive to mass public expectations. It's a rare occurrence in the arch of an aging female that is nearly free from failure potential.

A 25 year old woman who knows this, who can sling her unattached, unsettled, unwashed up life over her back and jog down the streets, is a blaze through the humdrum of society. A 25 year old woman who knows this is palpably, undeniably, alive. And the sad men can smell it with their needy little noses. Here is my conclusion on the myriad of ages that feel like they have a key to the life of a young woman:

I do not think that most men are delusional enough to believe their shouted vulgarity at a woman is going to be fruitful; I think they often know that it is a futile device as it relates to a means of intercourse. Rather, I think this age gap sexual harassment comes from their attempt to reallocate my power to themselves and thusly to escape the respective ailments of their various ages/life stages. They try to do this by making an emboldened, unattached, vibrant young woman scared, startled, and mostly: objectified. I mean objectified in the most potent sense. The harassment is an attempt to remove my mobility. Power and potential energy both become completely unthreatening when made stagnant. I can't usurp them if I'm glued to the floor in fear of them. This niche motivation for attack grows in the young and the old men by using their own insecurities as food. The young men are afraid that I am occupying too much of the space that they are preparing to inhabit; that there will not be room for them. The old men see in me the power and influence in society that they've lost. (I'm only talking about the old and young men who are harassing 25 year old women…I'm not saying that all young men are afraid of female dominance in their future progression nor am I saying that all old men have lost power or are bitter about it).

Filtering the never-ending-flow of sexual harassment through this awareness changes nothing, but it does give me a life vest. That take-it-on-the-chin attitude that originally concerned me, is actually my survival tactic. When the comments, gestures, and physical attempts by these men fail to make it into my body but instead ricochet off me, I maintain my glorious power and keep moving. The sad men get hit with their own failure when their violence boomerangs back to them without grabbing any of my potential or joy. They are their own grim

reaper and I am not obligated to dispel their self
destruction.

AFTERWORD

Here's the plain truth to how and why this was written.

How:
For 9 months, I had a strict no tears in front of boys rule. I made no proclamations. No commitments. I told none of them any of my feelings. No long messages. No impassioned fits. No questions about meaning of interaction. No future planning. I wrote it all down instead. I was endlessly mirroring their detachment. I was trying on a version of the male experience that looked alluring.

Why:
I wanted to earn back the sole ownership of my own attention and effort. I wanted to unwrap every finger that curled around me as a tether to a person instead of a purpose. I was determined to enforce that I develop my self instead of lay down my life to aid the progression of another man.

Caveat:
Some things were gained, many were loss. I can't help but wonder what would be different if I had let myself cry at least on one occasion.

Dedicated, retrospectively and sincerely, to the innocence of all my subjects.

CREDIT WHERE IT IS DUE

[my list of co-authors]

what do a:
midwest-transplant photographer,
all-nonsense soccer player,
drummer from my favorite band,
rock climbing filmmaker,
pilot with bleached hair,
anarchist motorcyclist,
skinny jean clad model,
sports car driving cowboy,
vintage playboy magazine collector,
not-so-gentlemanly scholar,
statuesque entrepreneur,
aged out soft boy,
gorgeous barista,
bi-lingual climate scientist,
carpenter with 2 art degrees,
sparkly-eyed investor,
mullet-rocking-international-picnic-partner,
& skate-boarding actor
have in common?
this book.
thanks for the plot points, boys.
(you've been excruciatingly adored)

i love you! i like you! i detest you! xx

I HAVE TO GO NOW

[goodbye]

Made in the USA
Monee, IL
15 March 2023